EVERYTHING IS STRANGE

Also by Frank Kuppner from Carcanet

The Intelligent Observation of Naked Women
Ridiculous! Absurd! Disgusting!

EVERYTHING IS STRANGE

Frank Kuppner

CARCANET

First published in 1994 by
Carcanet Press Limited
208-212 Corn Exchange Buildings
Manchester M4 3BQ

Copyright © Frank Kuppner 1994

The right of Frank Kuppner to be identified
as the author of this work has been asserted
by him in accordance with the Copyright,
Designs and Patents Act of 1988
All rights reserved

A CIP catalogue record for this book
is available from the British Library
ISBN 1 85754 071 9

The publisher acknowledges financial assistance
from the Arts Council of Great Britain

Set in 10 pt Palatino by Bryan Williamson, Frome
Printed and bound in England by SRP Ltd, Exeter

Contents

you died of cancer –
so what –
you are still more important than cancer.
(15.8.21 – 16.3.93)

Last Eternal Moments

1
No, thanks. I'd rather have another Universe.
Something a little brighter, if you don't mind.

2
Blood is another object not impossible in the universe;
As is a red dress, draped over the back of a chair.
What a huge sound a cup makes, knocking against a saucer!

3
I think this book is nearer 70 than 60 years old.
A tiny insect is crawling over page 174.
Could it fly if it wanted to? I rather doubt it.
Does it even know whether it can fly or not?
Whichever it is, I doubt that all the more.
I find the text moderately interesting.
Each day, most days, I read a brief portion more of it.
As, for instance, in this dull, grey, unenterprising,
But for the moment astonishingly modern morning.
Is this nonentity really the leading crest of Time?
This silent moment – with a freebooting insect
Marauding over some words Cicero wrote
Less than a year before his death (I think)
Noticeably more than two millenia ago?
He stretched his neck out, the more quickly to be killed.
Some obliging unknown man then killed him quickly.
Strange: to kill Cicero, and *still* not have your name remembered.
I flick the insect off the page, and resume my reading.
I have not the least idea where my victim fell.
Nor whether it was still alive or not as it did so.
The dull light floats me a little further forward.
So much for two inhabitants of the universe, eh?
Now: what was it Epicurus said regarding pain?

4
Throw your toys onto the floor.
Abandon your game spectacularly,
And put on exquisite adult clothing.
Move about my room with a rare grace,

9

Accustomed by now, I suppose, to being a woman.
After all, we must learn the truth some time.
And if we do not learn the truth some time,
We shall die without ever learning it, I suppose.

5
Meanwhile, the duck, which once thought whatever it thought,
Before a Chinese cook so expertly treated its carcass,
Will very soon be adding to the pulsing chaos
Of the numerous progeny of our interiors.
Hordes die every second, unsuspected, in our bloodstreams;
Millions of them. Millions. Millions. And not only in the
    bloodstream.
Your eyes sparkle. Are my eyes sparkling too?
Children must be sleeping not very far from here.

6
Another morning. More people with dangling penises
Are killing each other in the name of Infinite Powers.
I'll probably go to the library again this afternoon.

7
I lean against the window on the sixth floor of a library.
What am I reading? What does it matter? I look out
Over a more or less familiar cityscape,
Filled with familiar buildings placed at odd angles.
Something terrible is happening tomorrow.
Something, from my point of view, barely conceivable;
Involving a woman whom I have thought about
Innumerable times in the last year or two or three,
And a man who seems (to me) to be wholly superfluous.
It seems to be happening. It does seem to be happening.
While, in the distance, sunlight picks out a raised part of a
    motorway;
Where three changing lines of cars are travelling towards me,
And three changing lines of cars are travelling away from me.

10

8

An exhibition of pictures of extinct
Or severely threatened birds fills a long space
In the gallery. I have looked at most of them,
As casually as a guaranteed immortal,
Before I realise I am not really looking –
But still am drifting slowly through the memory
Of something unforgettable that happened two days ago.
I am already confident it shall prove to be unforgettable.
Can I really have, since then, experienced two full days?
A grim, double eternity, under the circumstances.
Without ever having concentrated, I reach the end.
Should I retrace my steps for a closer look?
After all, we so very nearly have something in common.

9

The Universe lasts in all for about a minute.
Although sometimes it can seem like a minute and a half.

10

Hand me over that decade, would you, darling?
I would like to observe it from a little closer to.
It is holding up remarkably well, all things considered;
Despite the oppressive integrity of its silence.
Now hand me over that small bra of yours, will you?
That's right. Directly across this impossible space.
Now: close your gorgeous eyes, and count slowly to thirty.
No, of course I'm not going to do something dirty.

11

Once again in the main road just before noon,
Following my normal, unimportant pursuits,
I glance across to the busy sidestreet which leads,
Eventually, after a slope and a slight turn,
To the house where she is living. To my astonishment,
Expecting only a chaos of cars and people,
I see above the roofs a perfect bright half-moon.
An otherworldly, undeniable visitor;
With no sense of intruding in the wrong place.

11

I am almost as shocked as if I had seen her face.
But that is for other people, at the moment.

12

Thanks to an explosion perhaps eight billion years ago,
We hurry towards a train; and we catch it just in time.
How surprised they will surely be to see us this afternoon!
(Not unreasonably so, under the circumstances.)

13

Truly, in the four-fifths of an eternity
in which hydrogen, its derivatives and its predecessors
have whistled outwards, combining and recombining;
in the billions of years in which chaotic gases and liquids
gave the earth innumerable unseen surfaces;
in the unimaginable tempests of the unimportant sun;
in the slow drift of unsuspected vibrant species to land;
in the huge rock-crystals that hurl negligently past nearby;
in the tiny crystals which can change us utterly;
in the inextinguishable heat which shrieks and rampages
somewhere away beneath that most elegant footwear
discarded beside a bed, upon which a woman
lies, laughing, as she reads out something absurd from a
        magazine –
so devastating a complex pattern of simple sounds –
that this shy hill, whose crest we help to populate
is instantly revealed to be the living centre
of Time and History and Joy and Musicality –
and Something Else even greater – what is it called?
Oh, keep talking; keep talking until I can remember.
Another four-fifths of a second should be all I need.

14

But if you too lived on a huge stone hurtling through the sky –
Much of it an explosion – what would you believe?
What would it be right to believe, in such a predicament?

12

15
What did they want? What did they think they wanted?
They are all dead. What would they have preferred?
Were they fairly treated? Did they cry for a long time?
If so, how far away are they now in the sky?
If not, how far away are they in the sky now?
But what sky is there, except this same sky here?
And I could lie in your garden, watching these clouds
For longer, longer, and longer. Such special clouds
To float so directly above your abandoned towel.

16
The day after the last day will be of quite staggering beauty.
Rather like the whole Universe waking up in your bed;
To find itself looking at an imitation antique clock
Which you must surely have chosen for yourself.
Will loud footsteps also be disappearing on the nearest street?

17
Ah yes. Innumerable are the places that I
Would like to visit. Too many to list, or hope for,
Or even remember the names of. As, for instance,
The village where my father was born; Lascaux;
And a room I have never seen – a presumably glorious room,
Somewhere within a normal building ten minutes walk from here,
Which I hurried past this morning, expecting nothing,
And then again in the afternoon and evening,
Like a man who had not the least idea where he was.

18
The sound of a father playing gleefully with his daughter –
Or is that his son? I cannot be quite sure –
Reverberates noisily through my dull beige ceiling
From the room directly above. Only now,
Having stopped reading, do I become aware of it.
I put down on the table a book purchased last week,
In which, among so many Chinese details,
In rain falling more than a thousand years ago,
A man is glancingly reminded of his native village.

19

A fairly normal day – the tall gent in Room 6
is playing rubbishy music with his habitual loudness;
so that the monotonous repetitive drumbeats
win their way through, maddeningly, into my own abode.
And, turning from one form of penetration to another,
through the wall to my left, the modest elderly couple
who make occasional appearances during the daylight hours
on a principle which I cannot even surmise,
are now, to judge from a usual repertoire
of sighs and grunts, heading for the ultimate bliss.
The bright cold light contains the voices of children
shouting in a nearby school – where, thirty years ago,
I too was a pupil, now sitting as I am
in front of a gas-fire; somewhat disappointed
to have yet again received no letters today,
and leafing desultorily through a book about free will.

20

Of course children play among the hyper-explosive stars.
Where else are they supposed to play, for heaven's sake?
Even so; I wish they might at least go into the lane.
I mean, they are interrupting important trains of thought.

21

Another morning, and letters continue to scurry
over most of the globe, in terrifying profusion;
over-compensating for the doubtless soon to be resumed
millenia of utter terrestrial letterlessness.
Odd, all this communication in the vast dark.
That I lay awake for so much of last night
now seems to have been rendered hideously irrelevant –
thinking and rethinking of one particular woman's actions,
torturingly intermingled with her inactions,
who once again this morning has not yet written to me,
perhaps to tell me how she might once more be reached,
or at least to enclose some helpful, discarded underwear.
However, even now her letters might be travelling
to unknown destinations and their fortunate recipients;
possibly at the other end of the earth;

possibly to a near neighbour in this street.
I read my latest postcard from Switzerland anyway,
and, within ten minutes of receiving it,
I pin it to the normal wall. There it shall stay
for the next few dozen days, so I suppose,
through morning after morning of lengthening silence.
Eventually, the silence will prove to be unbreakable.

22
Can't someone force time, or merely the world, to behave
    properly?
You kiss a woman's ----, and she then marries someone else!
That may even have been her you passed in a busy lane this
    evening.

23
Very well, my darling, let me answer your question seriously,
Since you persist with it in that unignorable voice.
I shall leave brilliance to more appropriate occasions.
As I find myself doing more and more often nowadays.
No. I do not wonder who else I might have been, if not me.
Those who were not conceived are not non-existent people.
They are not even 'those who were never conceived'.
They are nothing. There is no such they in existence.
At most they are possibilities which exist, or once existed,
In more than one object scattered throughout real space.
You are puzzled that I so love certain photographs.
But all the ingredients needed for photography
Existed long before photography itself appeared.
The dispersed ingredients are not the thing itself.
The incipient human being, likewise, arrives only at conception.
Before that, there are only possible constituents,
Variously disposable within different agencies.
How else, anyway, *ought* we to be elaborated?
A characterless sperm outstrips such millions of others,
And gets so subtly to a tiny point first; even though
Still you are nowhere, even you, until that initial impact,
And so strange a presence directly after that moment.
But look: we have somehow developed beyond that moment.
We may possibly face each other across a table,

15

A table resplendent with china, light and newspapers;
And that we emerged from infinitesimal, intricate tubes
Should be accepted as true; for, amazingly, it *is* true.
After all: where else is love supposed to emerge from?
What other way ought there to be of producing it?
For our emotions must develop from real physical objects,
However subtle they grow, however rich, however all-pervasive,
Unless we are to be satisfied with merely imaginary love.
And my love for you is not an imaginary love.

24
After trickling through various gardens,
And disappearing beneath a road, the streamlet
Piddles its way out of a wide culvert,
Meanders thinly over a broad beach,
And, if the tide is out, exhausts itself
In a large, apparently-never-growing puddle,
Nondescript among pebbles, mud and shingle;
Or, if the tide is in, it absent-mindedly
Wanders serenely off into the overwhelming sea.

25
This is already the other world that you are in.
Any cloud could tell you that, if you watched it properly.

26
And so the nymph, waiting patiently at the taxi-rank,
Eager to take to a desperate person waiting for them
Kindness, understanding, various adorable
Orifices, and possibly even love –
Irritated by the relentless braying fatuity
Of a loud person next to her in the queue,
Silenced him with an expert flick of her wrist,
And suavely addressed him thus. Oh, very well.
Very well. Let me try again, since you insist.
It is not inapt that I should have to repeat myself
As far as I can. The point bears repetition.
All the same, it surprises me that you should find so elusive
The thought that any real thing must be one particular thing:

16

That particular thing, and not any other.
For nothing, whatever it is, is actually something else;
Not if we are talking of real, existing objects.
And insofar as anything is a particular thing,
By that very fact it cannot be made twice.
Two distinct examples of it simply cannot occur,
Any more than the same life can have two separate mid-points.
However similar one point may be to another,
You cannot have two instances of the one particular point.
Let me try to extend the point a little further.
Whatever was the process which made a particular thing,
Exactly the same process cannot repeat itself,
For the repetition of something is not the thing itself.
Even the repetition of the same act
Is not the same act as the same act it repeats;
For the second is a repetition, and the first is not.
Let me try to extend the point a little further.
After the extinction of life in your own body,
You cannot come back to life as the same person,
For the person in question has actually ceased to exist.
Nor can you come back after death as somebody else.
Only someone else can appear. And someone else,
It should hardly need to be said, will not be you.
Even the reconstitution of your own body –
Whatever feasible process such a phrase could possibly indicate –
Would provide only a replica of your body;
And a replica of a thing is not the thing itself.
I concede that this argument is none too original.
Lucretius pointed most of it out millenia ago.
But numerous different minds, combining into existence,
Then uncombining back into non-existence,
To provide the raw material for some other things –
Now that their interlude of puzzlement is over –
Have missed this rather simple point in century after century
    after century.

27
Morning. The clock is almost screaming with happiness.
God has evidently locked Himself into the bathroom with you.
Three inviting letters wait on the table to be opened.

17

28

A morning like this surely gives me the right to invoke them –
If anything does. All those people who were never created!
All those possibilities who were never realised!
Even though, of course, there cannot be such people –
What fascinating remarks would fill their treasured childhoods.
What stabs would hit them as unknown others entered a room.
What furtive, regretted acts they might even have committed.
And what children they too might have managed to produce;
Whom they would sit beside in kitchens very like this,
Planting warm, cautious kisses on those frail, somehow real
    skulls,
As a voice from the nearby television talked about coming
    storms.

29

We are (I hope) all familiar with that calmness
when the pain of a dental injection has at last
disappeared, as one always knew it would, yet somehow
never quite believed beforehand; and one no longer
touches the sore place with one's tongue, trying to gauge
how much more time must pass before the face
recovers the normal feeling of a normal face,
which is what, apparently, it used to have. In the next space,
if the recent, cryptic remark which she made in passing
is, as we say here, anything to go by,
and I have interpreted it correctly, someone
of inexpressible beauty is doing something
alas inexpressible in another way.
After she had left, noticing my calming jaw,
I picked up the pen on the table, and began writing
impromptu on the back of a defunct sheet of paper
of the sort which the bank seems to think itself qualified
to address to her. And I find that my thoughts turn,
as they so often seem to do nowadays,
to thoughts of extinction; which I find a fashionable –
albeit perhaps a merely transient fashion –
and genuinely interesting subject. For, although
if we don't all disappear now, we shall all disappear later,
whether tomorrow or in sixty years' time;
and our artworks will anyway wholly evaporate,

18

like the once so plentiful excrement of any number
of eliminated beasts; on perhaps a
correspondingly large number of planetary
surfaces; we would still prefer to wait a little,
by and large. So every pregnant woman
appears to possess a heartening faith in the future,
and the neighbours' children, when depression looms,
become, though scarcely likeable, yet at least
useful little loud bad-tempered arguments.
They suggest that things will continue; and she will return.
Not before time, I may add. Still absent. Still absent.

30
Out on a walk along Great Western Road,
I toss a letter I have carried too far in my pocket
into a sudden pillar box which I have never used before.
I have passed by it a few times in my forty years, I suppose.
Two days later, I get an answer from Dundee –
A city which I do not remember ever visiting.

31
Odd to think that this grey, windswept morning
Which starts off another, surely unnecessary week,
So bleak, so unconnected to all that went previous
That it might be the rootless first day of the entire universe,
Nonetheless is still filled by countless moving objects
Often lovelier than the creation of the world,
Which I dare not further characterise than by the word 'female'.
Such are the stray thoughts that sometimes console a worried
    man.
But the door of the public phonebooth where I wait my turn
Eventually opens, and a subdued figure vacates it.
A woman. A rather plain, uncaptivating woman,
Who has evidently just heard something worth thinking about.
I walk past her briskly, another expressionless human being.

32
Only after completing the perfectly humdrum phonecall,
Having retrieved my card from the public machine,

19

Do I notice the little pencilled cross on its upper surface.
I put it there myself almost two years ago,
Having just made a tremendously significant phonecall –
Fruitless and baffling, but tremendously significant –
To warn me not to squander this now precious object
On undeserving ordinary future usages.
All this I had forgotten when I stumbled across it
A few days ago, and slipped it into my pocket
Unthinkingly, happy to postpone an impending expense.
For two years it has lain about, unheeded, between phonecalls.
Between my talking, in two such different tones,
Trying to convey such different emotions,
To one woman in a January, and another in December.
Not even a contiguous December.
From streets at most five minutes walk apart.
Still only the same brief walk apart, needless to say.

33
The sound of a plane fades away over the roof opposite.
Half an hour since the voice on the telephone
Told me of my aunt's death. I stand at a window.
In one of the lit rooms visible across the lane
Two adults and two children are sitting round a table,
Their gestures so lively in the renewed silence.
What noise they must be making, from the look of things.

34
That the East has produced much of value hardly needs to be
        said.
But I doubt whether all its mystic wisdom put together
Is as miraculous as the very material workings of the telephone.
A slight noise, then devastating warm tones from a distance.

35
The slow movement of the Mozart two-piano sonata
continues to issue from the stereo cassette-deck,
which has a slight imbalance between its speakers –
the left being privileged – as I look up
from a not particularly good book about Zen

by someone called Eugen Herrigel, realising
that my father and mother, at present in the small
and not overwhelmingly famous town of West Kilbride,
southwards along the coast, are both still alive,
and merely doing some shopping. Somehow this seems
an almost unbearable success. A light breeze disorders
the treelet (whose genus I must try to find out)
in the brief garden beside the road, and I
reflect for a moment about how little I know
of my father's complex and baffling itinerary
during the last war, over four decades ago;
deciding that the details will probably escape me
forever, as I glance down again to relocate
some moderately interesting remarks about Japanese acting.

36
Having switched the lamp off at night in the large low attic
Of my parents' house, I turn back to the pillow,
And almost at once grow aware of a brightness
Curiously enveloping me. My alerted eyes
Seek out the small skylight somewhere beyond my head;
And there, caught so neatly, hangs a huge full moon.
So much light, so much light; such a ridiculous amount of light
To be propagated across a near-empty near-infinity,
Through oceans of fine dust, to be intercepted
Somewhere halfway along a modestly important road
In a not particularly important town on a coastline.
I maintain my ever more locked gaze, until
It seems it is simply a lack of confidence prevents me
From reaching out slowly into the narrow darkness
As if to an elegant, sleeping face nearby,
And touching an utterly distant forehead for reassurance.
However, time will pass, and one falls asleep
Whether beside live foreheads or dead planets,
And mornings eventually follow of widely different characters.
In these, one may very well be extremely alone.
Or the door of the room directly underneath may open,
While various parents casually emerge from it,
Adding normal words to an already normal morning.

21

37

The mind cannot encompass all the important silences at once.
Newer vacancies jostle against so many of their predecessors.
Other pleasant breakfasts are no doubt being prepared
Elsewhere than in this friendly, agreeable kitchen,
Where I sit talking to a very close relative,
Our words interspersed with long, amiable silences.
But even to be surrounded by voices which one loves
Is not always to be surrounded by the right voices.
There are still necessary and desired elsewheres being occupied,
Where the wrong clocks agree to signal the correct time,
While the wrong mail drops through the nearby letterbox.

38

Between one heartbeat and another, what disappears?
Something usually too insignificant to notice.
To wit, the entire previous state of the Universe.

39

Smoke floating above the sea, as if it were
A more leisurely sort of bird. A sort of bird
Not quite realised in the wheeling forms
Which, on our roofs, make such unattractive noises.
We waken up, and the smoke of dreams drifts out
Into the bright neat room, as if it were
Only a sharpness which the air takes on
In yet another ordinary morning.

40

Each dawn need not happen. But it does.
And when it doesn't, something else happens instead.

41

Likewise, a corpse is one more possibility of nature.
And Grief is something else which emerged in the Universe
During the internal redistribution of its components –
Like meteor showers, or undiscoverable rivers,
Or moments of angry silence in a million weeks.

22

That dazzling toss of the head! That moment of irritation
At a computation that proves strangely recalcitrant –
How many dissolved predecessors lie behind them!
While a cup beside you continues to emit steam,
As a star continues to work not too far beyond the window,
And I am almost certain that I am not quite dreaming.

42
Normally, on the first morning of the year,
A radio-programme of music is broadcast from Vienna,
Which I like to listen to, as a sort of spiritual exercise.
But though this abnormal morning had just such a beginning,
Somehow or other (sloth? sleep?) I managed to miss that
        programme.
Therefore, I failed to capture it on tape,
To add to the earlier examples which I have slowly accumulated.
Late in the afternoon, I take one of these out,
Feeling that the year has not yet properly begun.
I listen to very nearly the same Viennese music,
Greeted by overwhelming and similar enthusiasm;
The intoxicating optimism of another fresh start.
A rapturous seeing-in of a split-new year,
Already gathering dust off somewhere in the past.
I am not even sure how far in the past it sounds from.
Is that one year ago? Two years? Three years? More?
Dating optimism exactly can be a tricky matter.
Except for possibly informative announcements
Randomly preserved among the chunks of music
Precise identification is utterly impossible.
After a while, having heard all I need to hear,
I return the tape to its apportioned place,
Where it may well lie untouched for many further months.
I have still not chanced to learn what year's joy it was
Which I have just used as a harmonious substitute.
Real joy is real joy; that is the important thing.
Now I must go round to a friend's house, to help celebrate.
Well. I say 'friend'. That is perhaps not strictly accurate.

43

After much trouble in a complexity
Of corridors and stairways, the nymph at last
Locates the City Architect's Office, enters,
Crosses to where the relevant functionary is slumped,
Thoughtful, behind a desk. She sits down opposite,
Pulls out a notebook, and refreshes her memory.
The traffic flowing outside pretends to ignore her.
She smiles at a passing, silent thought. Then, crossing
Her sacred legs, without further preliminary,
She launches into the following genuine interrogation:
The buildings where we were born were never built, were they?
They were never mere plans, or merely half-constructed.
It seems they were always there. Always already there.
And, since we are much the same, that is surely appropriate.
Manufactures of impeccable timelessness,
We walk through them, or drift ethereally out of them.
We were not produced in any way at all, were we,
As a result of the somewhat crass activity
Of some probably not too well-known gent's penis. Were we?
With whom, perhaps, we long afterwards argued.
Or never saw. Or received superb advice from –
Possibly concerning the nature of the other sex.
Oh dear, no. Nothing as realistic as that.
That sort of crude materialism is not applicable to *us*,
Off whom the light reflects as clinically
As it does from the music-producing equipment beside us;
Below the piles of books by major philosophers,
Perhaps, produced by bloodless thinking machines.
Nothing to do with the seepage of fluids here.
Vaginas? Well, they are all very pretty, no doubt;
But one wouldn't exactly choose to be born from one, would one?
All far too blood-stained and undignified
For creatures of such immense spiritual sophistication;
So intent on grasping and transmuting the universe
Till it glows with a perfect, immaterial illumination.
But how do things look in the actual light? That is the first
    question.

24

44

Rain. Rain so brutally, unremittingly heavy,
It threatens to wash a morning right out of the calendar.
The two women whom I happen to be approaching
In the busy street where few (unlike them) have stopped
To talk for their own reasons, in the pouring rain –
I have never seen them before, I think – I am about
To pass them, quite without noticing, when the younger
Leans forward. The older does so in sympathy.
They briefly, lightly kiss – now so suddenly
Stretching similar features towards each other
Across a divide of generations, where decades
Of life are inextricably intertwined;
From a first cry, through many subsequent cries,
Modulating into years of shared expressions
Up to this rain-drenched point. I pass them instantly;
At first startled, then disconcertingly stirred
By that brief meeting of interrelated lips,
Before disappearing through a noisily swinging doorway.

45

It is not really happening – I am not really
Walking down this street, caught precariously
In a crossfire of sunlight and wind, towards
A relative whom I have not seen for years.
I am not quite waiting for these traffic-lights to change,
And the members of the crowd who break past me
On either side, with such odd resolution,
Are not quite in the thoughts of unseen, breathing figures.

46

How normally they stand out, talking, there in the garden;
Visible through the window, almost the same height;
Using language, I suppose, almost equally well:
Two large, complex thinking beings with small apertures
Through which other equal complexities sometimes emerge,
As the taller once emerged from the older figure.
Is it to pass by utterly unmentioned
That, last night, one of those seemingly normal creatures,
One of that pair of non-mythical beings talking in a garden,

25

Expressing herself no doubt with a certain forthrightness,
Or listening to the reply of a similar being
From whose intricate and equivalent construction
She emerged, a matter of decades ago now,
Into only this universe – no choice is offered –
Make the best of this one or go back to nowhere –
Sink back among the unrealised possibilities –
Infinite infinities of non-existent objects –
A single perfect step back to somewhere or other –

47
How can you argue seriously with someone whose c----- you
    have touched?
What strange routes we have come down to reach this public
    anger.
Can she really talk to her parents in the same tone of voice
    sometimes?

48
I see the main street has its usual crowd this morning.
I suppose I am forced to conclude it is only another real morning.
I suppose I may even buy another newspaper soon,
And read it as one reads an ordinary newspaper;
More struck than usual, perhaps, by the strange ill-timing
With which others vanish, through accident or age,
Having gathered together their full heaps of futile irrelevant
    years.
By now, she must have entered the building where she works,
With that soft perfect skin transcendently dry and unmarked.
But who are all these people standing so unconcerned near me?
If I gave a shriek of joy, would they even hear me?
We stand, all separately waiting at the same lights.

49
A glance up at the gently sloping, not unbusy
Street where she lives, as I hurry on foot along
The still busier street that hurries by beside it.
That tourist coach, parked on its crest, must stand
Within sight of her window. Yes! Of course it does!

And a group of astonished citizens from France or Switzerland,
Desperate for a glimpse of real civilisation
After all the ersatz nonsense they are forced to make do with at
    home,
Are no doubt even at this very moment,
While I walk by so near for a few seconds,
A few seconds away, but not seeing her –

50
Like a refugee from a markedly famous German
Poem, I hurry through an incessant rain,
Though possibly my memory is playing me false,
Carrying (a modernist touch) a vast umbrella
Of brown and yellow battered segments. I climb
A tiny stairway. I stop beside a door.
I wait there for as long (a scatter of seconds –
Each of them long enough for a life to be created or changed in)
As an uninvited interloper may reasonably dare;
Until the ludicrous pressure of such pretended normality
Drives me off, down the stairway, back to a road
Which surely no-one will ever adequately explore.

51
What numerous rooms I have caught myself saying your name
    in!
I have scattered it for many months throughout various cities,
And throughout numerous districts of the same city.
You too must have been in some of them, I suppose;
But never exactly in one of those exact places.
Not that callously ugly garden near a skyscraper;
Not that rich beautiful street full of blondes and sportscars;
Not that friend's dull kitchen, in some desperate moment
Of a needless morning, alone. Not here; not now.
Always you have been elsewhere, saying whatever you are
    saying;
Addressing whatever people you are addressing
By whatever names you choose to address them by.
Then they will often use your own name in reply.

27

52

I have started listening to music again
With an intensity that surprises me.
You may have crippled my heart, or whatever that was,
But you have done wonders for a jaded pair of ears.
For some reason, I have reclaimed Beethoven in particular
After many aberrant months of comparative indifference.
Are you listening to him at present? No; almost certainly not.
God knows, he wrote enough to give us a wide choice.
Thousands of people must be listening to him so variously now.
But why can I not be someone who is overhearing your voice?

53

When impossible events have proved themselves to be possible,
There is not much else can be done. Either, I suppose,
Jump out of the window, or go on living,
Hoping for a gradual descent to those normal days
Which once might seem to have threatened boredom, but now
Would form a sort of quiet threatened paradise
In which one might return, on a nonchalant pleasant evening,
To the room one had long occupied, only to find
It had changed ownership to someone else completely.

54

All deeds produce results, and most absences of deeds too.
I am sitting alone in this room because of real and unreal
    telephone calls.
In other rooms move the hands that I should be catching by the
    wrist.

55

Evening. Late in the evening. So, so late in the evening.
Almost a full hour later than I had guessed.
Has it stopped? For how long? For how much longer?
Twelve weeks ago, learning of a death, I wept briefly.
Today, learning of a birth, I wept for a long while.

56

This is a curious business – trapped in the house all day
while some virus goes on a rampant itinerary of
my own overheated interior, as an afternoon
throws up for admiration a rare pair of eyebrows;
and now, in the evening, while I try not to sneeze too much,
because of the soreness when (I think) my lungs
expand against my adjacent (I think) ribcage –
astonishing to discover that I do in fact have a ribcage,
(if that is what it is); that I, presumably,
have always had a ribcage, and am not filled
by neat clinical diagrams, or a perfection
of stainless-steel impeccable machinery,
but a subtle supple soft excitable mess,
bits of which can hack against other bits –
I hope this digression is not too ferociously technical –
and now one channel of the television
shows a fine pair of 1985 Austrian breasts
in a film about business corruption is it, while another
shows an even finer pair of 1986 Hungarian breasts
in what may possibly be something to do with war –
doubtless a denunciation – but the nobler details
were all a bit of a blur, except the busts,
and I soon abandoned them; sitting, sniffing,
wondering about the contents of my own equivalent torso,
a slightly more modern one, but far less capable
of generating enchantment, rather than malevolent life.
Life, eh? What an invention. Excuse me while I cough.
It may all be better tomorrow. Or worse. Or much the same.
I refuse to be silenced merely by almost unendurable pain.
There's a copy of Marcus Aurelius here in the room somewhere.

57

Who would have expected another graveyard here?
At least the fourth so far in our brief perambulation
Of this historical town. How many of our private
Carefully selected streets seem to involve graveyards!
No. Please go on talking about the film you saw yesterday.
It interests me that you find it of interest.
We follow the long wall, on the other side of which
Compartmentalised scatterings of bone now rest in peace.
Did none of them also ever plan voyages to Greece?

29

58

Curious, the precision of this foreign country.
The ranks of newspapers outside its sunlit kiosks.
People who stand, exchanging the wrong consonants,
Then move off suddenly down different streets.
Let us follow any one – this one, for instance.
Let us follow him down this street, and up this stairway.
Let us watch him take a key out of his pocket,
Open the door with great ease, and go through
Into a house with which he is perfectly familiar.
Let us hurry out of a nearby kitchen to greet him,
Our beautiful face combining thoughtfulness and chic.
He plants a benign, somewhat absent kiss on this cheek;
Then goes off into his study, unfolding a newspaper.

59

Through the neighbouring wall, the sounds of two voices reach
　　me.
One of them is a visitor's; the other, my mother's.
I smile, fold over the newspaper, and continue to read.

60

Perhaps life is a background music playing in the foreground
So incessantly that we find it difficult to hear.
We scan the remote horizon for something exquisite and near.

61

A charming soft low voice crept up behind me,
And whispered: do you mind if I ask you a personal question?
Why is it so insulting to be only a part
Of a real, limited universe? What else could anything be?
Anything which is the product of real objects and events
Must be the product of in some way limited objects and events.
How else can one be acted on, but by circumstances
Which actually exist? Which are this rather than that;
Lying one way rather than all ways; slow rather than fast;
Or fast rather than slow; hot rather than cold;
Music rather than silence; oxygen rather than gold.
Listen: anything real is composed of actual details.

30

A particular composition of particular details.
Why this vast, abiding shame about the actual world?
The Universe is shunned like a guilty family secret.
But anything real must be part of something real –
Unless it is in fact everything. And few of us,
For all our inbuilt positional megalomania,
Are prepared to go quite as far, in a literal sense, as that.
So the people we meet cannot help but be the people
From that part of the universe we are travelling through.
For, if they were not, how could we ever meet them?
What other sort of being could anyone ever meet?
Perfect, unlocated, transcendental automorphs,
Wholly devoid of circumstantial detail,
Do not and cannot exist. Where could they be?
It would flout their composition to be actually anywhere.
It would not be good enough, even if it were possible,
To be manufactured outside the Universe –
Which is to say, surely, outside of everywhere –
Then squeezed in wherever appropriate, as if
The cosmos were a sort of large box with a hole in it,
Which life, or something else, could be forced in through from
    outside.
At which point the nymph stopped talking. She blushed deeply,
Gave a brief curse, then rushed out into the hallway,
Letting an incomparable silence descend on the small room
Which only the newborn child – but enough of this for the moment.

62
Merely because something of infinite value is now so near,
And we do not nearly understand how it can be so near;
Emerged at length from such a tangle of possibilities
Which the understanding loses itself in seeking to follow;
The remote galaxies have not become less numerous,
Nor the objects which may be bigger than the galaxies,
Whether remoter or imperfectly realised by us,
Who, after all, fail to realise so much,
Even this inexhaustible small world before our eyes.
Certainly, the unbelievable astronomy books
Remain on sale in the shops, and on view in the libraries.
Each of our discoveries would surely dwarf us further
If size were the same thing as significance.

31

But, if size were the same thing as significance,
Why would that tiny object dressed in miniature clothes,
Clothes that hardly seem bigger than the idea of clothes;
Why would that small object, which you hold in your arms,
That tiny object, lost in its own dreams,
Not yet knowing whose body it is clutched against,
Whose beautiful, enchanted, productive body;
Why would the least, sudden, gratuitous shift of its head,
Which it can move through such impossible distances,
Such vast, spasmodic, untrackable distances,
Thrown out from next to nothing, into such distances
Which can somehow be contained in this normal room,
This normal room in a city full of rooms?

63
What? Were you really once a child; really and truly?
Show me the entire universe in a half-filled blue cup.
Like that cup on the table beside your ten-year-old hand,
In a photograph which your adult hand now reaches out towards
     me.

64
What will you next open those impossible eyes to see?
What can we offer you worth such perfect beauty of detail –
You, who do not yet know what universe this is.
Indeed, we ourselves are far from perfectly well-informed.
We had already supposed there must be infinite amounts
Not to be understood by us, and then you came,
To raise the infinite universe by another infinity;
Another unfathomable dot among the skies.
For where else could you be, if you were not here?
Even behind your closed eyes, you are here and only here.
And what you next observe, perhaps, doubly fortunate,
Will be the huge eyesight from which you derive your own,
Since beauty can somehow split into plural beauty.
At least for a little longer, you will be spared the sight
Of ruined buildings, where quiet, hurrying travellers
On their way to work, or returning to their children,
To their defenceless, open-eyed and so adored children,
Are ripped to pieces for some political fantasy

32

Which blinds a few dozen to the sight of what murder is;
Or of some ridiculous, roaring, disinhibited crowd,
Rampaging among a complex range of electrical marvels,
For the sake of some wholly self-destroying fatuity
Involving belief in a future life; a life
Somehow beyond, somehow richer, somehow greater than this,
This existence here, this impossibly full existence,
Which seems to have permitted this small, precious grouping,
Where one may be held in the arms, and be whispered to;
May be handed over hypercautiously to someone else;
May be watched hugely, lest it vanish into the air;
May be taken back with a sigh, another effect of the air –

65

Though once you pushed, pushed, desperately pushed;
And a child's head painfully, unbelievably emerged –
Two years on, you talk to me gaily outside a bank –
In this street full of talking, alert heads –
The child, I suppose, yawning in a room somewhere nearby –

66

Oh, what is not contained here in this small room!
Just kick the Sombrero Galaxy behind that chair.
Or whatever it is. One of your dropped shoes?
Let me put back in the drawer underneath the window
This object here – what is it? A useless knife,
Or perhaps the History of the Development of Thought.
It is clearly one or the other. What is that noise?
Have you reinvented the lost music of the Greeks,
Or are you asking me about the evening meal?
Oh, the scent of European Civilisation –
Perhaps even more! – drifts in from the kitchen.
If I could only purée the entire Universe,
It might just yield the proper adjective for what we now feel,
Wrestling with God or the too tight lid of a pickle-jar,
While Eternity lightly wrinkles her glorious troubled eyebrows.

33

67

I follow you nonchalantly past a lightly opened doorway.
What a huge, astonishing sight I glimpse on the other side.
Is the Andromeda Galaxy really bigger than your bed?
I suppose it must be. How terribly impressive.
Was someone really asleep there a few bare hours ago?

68

A trio of youths outside a shop mock the shape of my beard.
Their cruel laughter reaches upwards into the air, and vanishes.
The air extends further, until it too vanishes.
Soon there is only the darkness of space, with occasional little
        dots in it.

69

A single huge leather bag floating through space.
Well, something has to be there if not us, I suppose.
Her sky-blue bag hangs from the chair opposite me.
The snow falls exactly onto the pavement outside.

70

Ah! The long mute emptiness of space is broken here –
Or, at least, it was here only a minute ago –
By a vast, rotating, slowly dripped together pebble.
And, for a few seconds in its day or so of existence,
On odd, largely silent, non-liquid bits of its volume,
Quaint bipeds inhale and exhale various gases
Without particularly noticing that they are doing so.
Some of which are disagreements about why they might be there;
Some of which are unequalled declarations of love;
Some of which are thrilling political shrieks;
Some of which are mature, gnomic shafts of understanding;
Some of which are infinitesimal hidden sighs,
Emitted for an unknown reason during sleep
By someone whose near silent head moves and moves,
Visible in the dim light of a digital clock,
Operating in a manner which I do not quite grasp –

34

71
On how many nights have you lain beside that man?
I lie awake, torturing myself by my own imagination.
I could ask myself, what are you doing, in a house not far from
    here.
I struggle not to think of what it is you might be doing.
Let me think of nothing but sleep. Nothing but sleep.
Your sleep. His sleep. No: even that is too much.
How can the Universe let you lie asleep beside someone else?
Why does it not intervene, spontaneously,
To correct this so obviously idiotic arrangement?
I could switch on a light, and look at a red curtain;
The back of a chair, a picture of a cup;
Even, in the tiny distance, a photograph of you.
Yet someone else, not twenty streets from here,
Could turn on a light and see that face itself.
What emotion do you think this is? Guess anyway.
Or am I the only one who must guess such things?

72
Such an enchanting semblance of compassion
Was the late beautiful light among the autumnal trees,
Casting leafy shadows onto its playing children
Like a loving warm relative, anxious to protect them;
While their mothers stand in the street, talking in clear tones,
And letting their legs be admired with great subtlety.
Oh, clearly, there is nothing that belongs here more than we do.
Yet, what does any star really care whether it is shining
On 13 lifeless planetoids, or merely upon 12?
Is the 13th also there, not yet devoid of life?
Are there philosophers on it, trying to devise
Proper rules for conduct? Are there numerous bodies
Being slaughtered or merely coerced in tribute to
Dazzlingly imaginary Gods? Are its grandmothers
Gazing tearfully at brand-new precarious children?
Are there people sniffing in untidy sunlit rooms
As they jot down brief remarks about possibilities of lifelessness?
Here? There? Where? What does it matter?
Nothing matters more, of course – but what does it matter?
And if it mattered more, what would that too matter?
Some worry that the world may possibly have no point.

35

Others are drawn to a somewhat intenser question:
What could possibly be the point of having a point?

73
Very well. It will soon be time to leave.
Your father walks pensively across the room,
A wise, tense man with a lifetime's experience;
By now, I would guess, incapable of breaking into a run.
You derive in part from a transient shiver of his body.
Even those priceless legs, which still may run when they need to
The least grain in his coffee-cup is bigger than what you once
    were.
Or what he once was, if it comes to that. Or me too.
Oh, these teasing, unoriginal thoughts about origins!
Some male approaching some female, not so long ago,
(Or let it be her approaching him, if you prefer;
The exact sequence of moves is not the point at issue),
And you still nowhere; or me; or whoever it is –
Except that no 'whoever it is' is there yet;
Only so many possibilities distributed
In tiny particles ascending or descending
The adjacent coils of intricate interiors
In a manner rather too hard to contemplate.
For the thought of one's father's ---- in an excited state
Is not something one likes to dwell upon,
However nearly one once dwelt within it.
In fact, so unattractive is such a prospect
That most, I suppose, never face the thought at all.
Where you are concerned, there is even less seductiveness.
To think of him approaching some smiling woman,
And you still nowhere, even when the caresses start!
Odd, to have so much difficulty in coping with
What one cannot even begin to deny was necessary.
Odd, but for human beings a remarkably common state.
Odd too, to watch your father come into the room,
Talking to you nonchalantly about air-travel,
As if all of us had always been this size,
This habitual weight and bulk and spaciousness;
Rather than, say, each tinier than your ----,
That priceless central detail, so easily overlooked,
Which somehow he was able to help have developed

36

From a roughly equivalent structure now utterly absent,
So that, a filling slice of a century later,
A complete stranger, from a wholly different place –
(After much thought, I remove a dozen or so lines.)

74

Is there always another child perhaps; the child you did not have?
The third child, perhaps, of the family with two?
The second child, likewise, of the family with one?
The only child of the childless couple, who find better things to
    do?
Or perhaps they are mute and devastated by its absence.
The planet spins on its way, anyway, slightly flattened at the
    poles.
So many schools release so many children each day,
But even from there, so near the moon, no-one hears their
    shouting.
No-one can see in which room in the same street
A childless person sits at a table writing,
Not far away from a picture of colossal stellar clouds;
While a neighbour helps a child with mathematics homework:
Aid being given to someone else who has also, somehow,
    arrived.
But by now the planet has moved slightly further, still flattened
    at the poles.

75

Yes, yes; believe in your God while he still has time.
Before the stellar clouds insist on a different local shape.
With what speed the planet hurtles through unbounded space.
This second. Now this second. Not this second? And off –

76

Some think God tortures us because he loves us so much.
What a shame he does not hate us, and treat us kindly.
Thus: every evening, regularly, for six or seven years,
The inoffensive and devout middle-aged woman
Lights a candle in front of a favoured religious image,
And prays intently. I do not know what for,

37

But it was not for this. One night, the candle
Catches the hem of her highly flammable nightdress,
Envelops her in flames, and burns her to death.
Thus she is taken off to meet her God of Love,
Possibly with a ready question on her lips.
Let us hope he was wearing some means of identification.
He could so easily be mistaken for his opposite number
By anyone who judges character in the light of actions.

77

What we disappear into is neither light nor darkness.
What we disappear into is merely disappearance.

78

Look. This here is the Universe. There is nothing behind it.
Nor is there anything in front of it.
The great trembling secret behind all existing things
Is only the existence of existence itself.
It is not something else, existing behind existence.
Behind existence, there is only non-existence,
Which is also in front of it, and on either side of it –
Or would be, if it existed. Which it does not.
That which seems to lie behind all religions,
Making them sound vaguely some chord of a great music,
Is merely the actual existence of life itself.
It is exactly the same thing that lies behind everything else.
Anything additional is more or less imaginary.
No single vast cosmic force unites all religions.
If one did, no doubt it would be human gullibility –
Unless we prefer the claims of megalomania.
Our Gods are our own echoes mistaken for other voices.
Each believer misinterprets in his own way the silence of heaven.
For we are producing voices in the skies,
Who were ourselves produced by the actions of the skies;
And to mistake chance noises for a voice
Undervalues the rarity of real, undeniable voices.
Oh, when shall I ever hear your glorious real voice again?
Yes, yes. It emerged from an infinity of unlikelihoods,
But the very next call this morning on the telephone,
That calm, miraculous object which clings to the wall of the
    hallway,

38

That Mozart of limpets, could bring it back to me –
Or traces of it sufficient to reassure me
That the disposition of matter in the Universe
Still balances in its present apotheosis.

79
Dawn. Some sort of starlight seems to be touching your face.
High gold clouds are clustered just above your body.
Will people still dare to produce newspapers today?

80
In a quiet afternoon, on the seventh floor of the library,
Among the numerous long rows of undisturbed volumes
Devoted to various aspects of religion and philosophy,
I caught sight of the nymph. She was in the next bay,
Elegantly disfiguring selected clamant textbooks
With charming little diagrams, most of them obscene.
What are you doing, I asked her, shocked to the core –
For I knew the answer at once. Do you not understand
That such behaviour could seriously compromise
Your status as a ticket-holder? Those warning placards
Attached to the walls and doorways leave little doubt of this.
She finished drawing a neat, intricate vulva
On a book about a great religious leader
(The second greatest ever produced, perhaps);
Replaced it, thus enhanced, on the shelves; turned round;
Gazed deep into my eyes; then slightly deeper –
And spoke as follows in a warm, melodious,
Deeply convincing voice. Listen, my overweight friend.
For millions upon millions upon millions of years the
        dinosaurs ----.
As did any number of defunct genera before and after.
A stratospherically exact number of such occasions
Available to the assiduous, omniscient researcher.
And every one of our great religions was still in the future –
Which is to say, nowhere – for the future is nowhere, as is
The diarrhoea which the plums will cause, before the plums are
        eaten.
For billions of years, no terrestrial had need of them.
How curious, then, that none of your great religions

39

Is more than .0002% of the age of the earth.
And none, I dare say, of our non-great religions either.
It shows you just how misleading statistics can be, doesn't it?
Here: this morning's newspaper provides further examples
Of the inexhaustible richness of Man's spiritual heritage.
Another few dozen, it seems, have been killed in that Indian
    town
Where a deity was once born in the form of an elephant.
Or was it a monkey? It was a monkey, I think.
Yes; the more I consider it, the more a monkey convinces me.
It has a pleasantly pseudo-Darwinian ring about it.
Perhaps another God was born nearby as a barrel-organ.
(For who are we to assign limits to his powers?)
I would suppose that, if God is to appear anywhere,
The most obvious place to do it would be China.
That China wasn't chosen seems itself sufficiently damning:
Our largest civilisation is there, waiting for him.
That would surely be the most predictable place to start.
Perhaps it goes against the grain to be so predictable?
Or perhaps, on second thought, he had little choice,
Given his unfortunate opinion of the pig,
But avoid a country where porkers are ubiquitous.
How thoughtful of God, to give us his opinion of the pig.
Which of us is not, after all, allergic to something or other?
But what a pity he failed to be equally specific
About some more contentious, metaphysical questions
Which have been argued over for year after year after year,
And not infrequently killed for. As far as I understand it,
We may cull this mighty lesson from many profound religions:
God has revealed innumerable vital truths to us;
But no-one can say for certain exactly what they are.
And now, if you don't mind, I'll take off my underpants.

81
Of course, one may find wisdom even in sacred books.
Just as, for instance, one may find a stray banknote inside one.
Neither, however, is something one can depend on.

40

82
Angels prefer to move in the other direction –
That much is fairly well-known – although the mechanism
Whereby this comes to pass is but imperfectly
Grasped. But I think I've caught a glimpse of the rules.
I think they are in fact fat corpuscles in
The bloodstream of a weeping God who wearily
Undresses for bed before a tv showing
A beauty talking to four political fools.

83
We swim, as I believe some dinosaurs did.
And I have followed you up a crumbling stairway
In a less than perfect tenement, watching
With what endearing care you tenderly
Exaggerated the natural sway of your hips.
Ah, these fashions! Let us hope they do not fade
Before we fade. I happily leave to others
Their superior prowess, their superior tailors.

84
Throughout the Peerless Book, God gives men warning after
        warning,
Telling them not to do what he has already ordained they shall
        do.
In a lesser personage, one would call this insanity.

85
God creates sinners, and then punishes them for their sins.
I suspect the Devil rather wishes he had thought of that one first.

86
Whenever you attack something which people think great,
They will usually respond that you are attacking greatness itself.
Don't you think, whoever you are, you ought to be more humble?
The true believer, for instance, is very very humble.
Having found the secret of the Universe, he can afford to be.

41

87

Perhaps only those who die on a Thursday afternoon,
With their face covered by that pair of their mother's underpants
Which she was wearing two hours before conception
Will experience the full bliss of life after death.
This cannot be less likely than most of the usual positions.

88

Pour out another cup of weak tea, and let us continue our
    journey.
But first, let us inspect the molten remains of this dead planet,
And see if we can guess how many Gods were once here,
In the minuscule band of time when such things were produced.
No. Useless. We have left it far too late, I fear.
Oh well. Another one to be scored off the list.

89

The Universe is wholly uninterested in applause.
Whenever applause stops, it has to continue anyway.

90

Evening in the library. Only another evening.
The world is not yet being finally destroyed.
Nearby, the hand of the clock again pursues
Its familiar route to the familiar number 8.
A thoughtfully sniffing man in a green jacket
Is noisily turning over the pages of a newspaper.
A slightly bored man is quickly writing down
This something or other on the back of a sheet of paper
Which requests money to train doctors abroad.
The world, once more, is not yet being finally destroyed.

91

A tentative golden light is caught by the window.
We hear a few details of an infinite story
Which has been spreading everywhere for billions of years.
We are given a few details to work upon;
And the strange thing is, we change it utterly.

42

We are smaller than one full-stop in any of these books
In this room which contains too many trivial books.
All our known universe is perhaps less than that chair.
Can I even begin to estimate how long I have had that chair?
The back is slightly broken, and I well remember
Already being bored with it five or six years ago.
How tensely she has gathered herself, a transient at its edge!
She moves her arms gently, to avoid alarming the cosmos.
And seeing the elegant watch lie so neatly on her wrist,
I find I am getting jealous even of Time itself:
An abstraction which some would claim does not even exist;
A mere interrelationship of objects which do exist.
Yet more torture at the thought of an imaginary rival!

92

After midnight, many sigh and locate their diaries.
We sit in buildings over a hundred years old,
Trying our best to remember anything we did yesterday.
The position of the stars would seem to be unchanged.
For a long time, the stars will seem to be unchanged.

93

We sit in the kitchen, making slightly awkward conversation.
But it seems ever more likely that we will get on all right.
Hectored to be on my best behaviour by someone
Whom the spasms of his penis decades ago made possible,
I do not tell him how beautiful his daughter's ------ is.
Nor do I exult that I am more familiar with it than he.
Or not explicitly so: such legendary savoir faire.
Two shy, solid men, we sit, talking of nothing.
Talking at some length, in fact, of the lane that runs nearby.
I wonder what he was kissing roughly thirty years ago.
Dear God: or what he was kissing even last week.
But the person hidden in the lane we do not talk about.

94

Which of our great-great-grandmothers is that,
Swaying inflammatorily down a narrow passageway,
Dazzlingly naked but for neat little boots,

43

To taunt a man who has seen three continents?
None of them? Are you sure? Are you quite sure?
How easily her progeny loses contact!
Why then does the man who is looking at her buttocks,
Barely able to repress a scream of triumph,
Wipe away a tear as he thinks of Japanese arbours?
Please do not say: nobody knows any more.
Not even if he is thinking of Japanese harbours?
Will no-one ever again turn the handle of that door?
Oh, all that planning in demolished buildings!
All that planning for what? Was it for this?
For me to watch that postcard near the window of your kitchen
Quiver a little in the surprisingly fresh breeze...

95
It is almost as if I am looking at the planet in person.
Let me try again to see if I understand.
If I keep repeating it perhaps I will understand.
Of the billions of sperms produced by almost any male,
Rarely will even a dozen be called upon for use.
And of the thousands of eggs which a female contains
Only at most a few hundred reach into the world beyond,
And few even of these are ever caught and provoked to expand.
Who, then, are these fatal crowds that we glimpse all around us –
Marching to commemorate blood shed seventy years ago;
Or seeking to cause more bloodshed as soon as possible,
Provoked by their full-blown fantasies about another world.
And who is this small object with miniature useable hands,
Whom we scarcely dare turn our eyes from for the least moment,
Lest somehow she vanish back into the vanished possibilities
Among the countless billions so impulsively left behind?

96
Curious. A thought-provoking colour supplement.
On one page, a young woman in saddling a horse.
Because of a drug taken by her mother when pregnant
she has no arms. She saddles the horse with her feet.
At the back page, another woman sits
on her luxurious couch, in her luxurious apartment.
One arm is touching a knee; another, resting on cushions.

44

The text describes her tireless struggle against sexist oppression.
Three large candles are glowing on the table beside her.
Who would not weep at the sight of the suffering of women?

97
It is difficult not to feel that, in some sense, health
is wasted on the healthy; ten minutes after
one has, in a strange town, encountered someone
whom one knows – someone, that is to say,
whom one has met and talked to several times before.
Her bicycle has disappeared over an exultant hill,
and now one is walking through an avenue of trees
where one used to meet one's sister, in those months
when her presence graced this town; swelling its population
for a moment as brief as the turning of that car-wheel;
and that car-wheel; and that car-wheel; though what country
they come from I do not know. However, glancing upwards,
I notice, at a window of one of the preconstructed
sheds sitting in the grounds of the Infirmary,
on top of another such shed, three nurses' heads,
all wearing uniform bonnets, and all laughing.
The leafy sunlight is joining in their joke.

98
Such rain; such wind; such further rain;
Such further rain; only the schoolchildren
Released for their dinner hour, seem not to notice it.
Slightly downhill, the chunky, highish church
Looks solider than ever; but how drenched
Its noble slabs are, glowing wetly,
Brilliantly, morosely, high up over the street.
And the ornate empty niches also, that decorate
The changing angles of the spire, seem now
Too frail to withstand one more assault like that just past.
Too strong a wind whips between their pillars.
The holy stone effigies are no longer there
On their high stone pedestals. Were they ever in place?
Or were they perhaps plucked out by passing waves,
Crashing to the ground, headfirst, on unseen sidestreets?

If so, for what reason? What would be adequate?
Clearly, that you have just passed! They lie in clusters
Of shattered stone, but joyfully, on those streets
Which the last day or so has heard you use;
Or they cling to the stonework near those windows which
You have recently looked out of. Cross to a window!
Gaze out! If it were really happening,
What shrieks, what cries of joy you would surely hear!
The fragments dance dizzily in the shocked city.
They leap joyfully down. They surmount the ridges
That make informal horizons in city streets.
Oh, long rows of the staggeringly bemused!
You pity them do you not? Or would you not?
Do tears perhaps fill your perfect neighbouring eyes,
As you look up in your centrally heated apartment,
Hearing the brave chorus of their distant, cracked voices
Disappear down the road beyond as they sing you
Their unutterably beautiful serenade, beginning
(For how else ought one to serenade the unutterably beautiful?):
'Try to be good, and try to expect nothing.
However, if you do receive anything, try to be grateful.'

99
Last night, a relentless heavy rain fell in my dreams.
I can't remember ever dreaming of rainfall like that before.
In the morning, beside a window, I fill a kettle at a tap.
Full heavy grey clouds lower outside, but the ground is still dry.

100
If you could be as happy as the thought
Of your happiness makes me, now, even on this
Evening of appalling downpour – no. It is night.
My hectic thoughts have somehow allowed it to get dark.
It is night; and you are on another continent.
Oh well. You are on another continent.
I take another small bite from an apple.
This universe contains apples and continents.
I bite an apple on a different continent.
Then a different bite on the same continent.
Someone who cannot possibly deserve to

46

Listens to your voice. Perhaps even your laughter.
I think, on the whole, I would rather you were not laughing.
Although, obviously, I do not favour your sadness.
Let me not think too closely what else you might be doing.
Why not just do nothing, whatever time it is there?
Is it not enough that he can simply see you,
And I can't? Not now. Not now. And not now either.

101

Morning runs along at your neat heels, shivering joyfully.
The future is continuing to plant its tiny, glorious seeds.
Lie for another fifteenth of a second on your bed.
The whole world will collapse and die of joy if you move too soon.
Please, please do not provoke it. Let it wait till you are gone.

102

So much nonsense about love duping us
Would only make sense if we did not belong
To these present circumstances; to this place and time –
As if we had merely floated in by mistake
From non-existence, and a wrong shrewd universe
Had glued us to the spot. Whatever depths
We find in each other's presence are real depths.
We are not measuring a world with the wrong tools.
Since no-one guides the world, we are not his fools;
Not brainless, storm-tossed sub-sub-subdivisions.
We are here, and it is up to us to decide.
And whatever we decide, they are real decisions.
Let us leave unreality to the unreal.

103

While revising a poem written long ago
In a condition of misery that I cannot wholly remember,
I remove the two exaggerated last lines,
Which consisted merely of the phrase, 'Not now',
Repeated ten or so times, with subtle alterations.
And all those grief-stricken moments are swept away with one
        cut!
Sent down the metaphysical disposal pipe

47

To join every great line that was never written.
As you can see, reluctant to let them go,
Curious to know their fate, I follow them a little way.
I stand at the edge of nothingness, peering in after them.
Everything else shall follow, of course. But not yet. Not yet.
Not yet. Not yet. Not yet. Not yet. Not yet.

104

I have finished the rich collection of classical aphorisms;
The fruit of so much thought by so many great minds.
I close the book with a sigh of deep contentment.
Why, five or six times, these people were even *right*.

105

Leaving the Book Festival for a brief break
between the various famous authors discussing imagination
and the evening session, when other famous authors
will discuss – what is it? – something else; to enjoy
on my own responsibility some of what remains
of a wonderful sunlit afternoon, I wander about
noncommittally at first, finding myself
trailing for no sure reason down Queensferry Street,
over cobbles and past a truly remarkable staircase,
following various noisy youths, who providentially
disappear somewhere while I am investigating
doorways, windows, houses, cars and paving-stones.
I start to cross a bridge, a magnificent high bridge
soaring above a barely discernible waterway,
beyond which might have been built a regal crescent
on the crown of a treelined hill. The houses are there,
but they face away; with delightful reassurance
showing only their mighty, uncaring backs to the vista
in a gesture, I hope, more of indifference than contempt.
While down below, half masked by all those trees,
there appears to be a sort of public garden,
beautifully tended and sparsely occupied.
In it, far off, a woman lies on her back,
in summery clothes, holding a baby. She lifts it
high above her, to the full extent of her arms,
shaking it. Despite the distance, the height, the traffic,

and the fact that she is ninety per cent inference,
it is perfectly clear to me that she is laughing.
Five seconds in the air; ten seconds in the air;
then brought back down to rest upon her body.
It seems I can even hear the child laughing too.
Such is the joy we may give to total strangers.

106   *Joy*
My mother beats the wall, letting me know that breakfast is
        ready –
while I stand, reading about some Byzantine emperors.
Unhurriedly, I go through to collect my plate.

In a Persian Garden

Being a radically altered version of that
Rubaiyat of Omar Khayyam which
Richard le Gallienne paraphrased 'from
several literal translations' before
the Great War. Here now thoroughly
revised, edited, rewritten and reordered.

The Le Gallienne version of *The Rubaiyat of Omar Khayyam* (from which I worked) contained 261 quatrains in all. Of these I discarded 129, and developed from the remaining 132 the present work of 150 verses. A dozen of these are, on my reckoning, entirely mine, and the same number entirely Le Gallienne's – although, in fact, I took over no quatrains *wholly* unchanged, feeling it necessary to fingerprint every one, however lightly.

At a rough estimate, some 60 per cent of the present wording comes from the original; some 40 per cent from me. However, of the 601 lines that follow, fewer than 80 will be found, bodily identical, in the earlier version, by whoever might care to look for them; and actual verbal alteration of one degree or other (ranging from the change of a single word to the provision of entirely new lines) occurs in three-quarters of them, quite apart from minutiae of punctuation.

Nor is the present order a passive derivation of the original. Thus, the first ten stanzas of the present version would, in Le Gallienne, have been numbered: 3, 2, 164, 228, 6, 225, 227, 97, 13 and 36. The last ten, for their part, would have run: 119, 119(?), 256, 242, 233, 223, 127, 14, 243 and 261. Thus, although an affinity exists, as indeed it should, it is a pretty independent-minded affinity.

The doubled final line of the present text marks the collaborative nature of the enterprise by giving both Le Gallienne's original version and a suggestion of my own, which rounds off the whole thing with an extended line.

1
Ah, Dawn is here! And, like a morning star,
The Sultan's palace glitters from afar.
No false mirage of morning, fair as dreams;
But stone, recalling us to what we are.

2
In Heaven's blue bowl the wine of morning brims.
A little cloud, a rose-leaf, in it swims.
The thirsty earth drinks morning from a glass
Whose sides are space and crusted stars its rims.

3
Great wheel that pauses not for all our cries –
How fair to look on are your morning skies.
Only at night I fear your placid blue;
I see such cruelty in those deep eyes.

53

4

Yet, with the morn, the wine-deserted brain
Feels all its riddles trooping back again.
What: am I sober when I find no answers?
And am I drunk when I see all things plain?

5

For some have luck, some gold, and some have fame.
But we have nothing, least of all a name.
Nothing but wine. That is: nothing but heaven.
The purest fire burns with the slightest flame.

6

When I am drunk with love the sky is clear.
I gaze deep into it, bereft of fear.
As I grow sober, I begin to dread
The shadows of those vultures drawing near.

7

The fiftieth cup makes me so wise with wine,
A thousand riddles clear as crystal shine;
And much I wonder what it can have been
That used to puzzle this poor brain of mine.

8

So in a tavern I pass half my days;
And sing, and drink, and give to God the praise.
Ready, at any summons of His voice,
To do His work in even harder ways.

9

Drunkards! So be it – yet, if all were wise,
All would be drunk like us, with dazzling eyes.
Poor sober world, day-long in misery.
Leave mosque and mart – come: join our Paradise.

10

Perhaps your Paradise beyond compare
Is some grim place of chanting, cold and bare –
But then, I never said my heaven was yours.
Wine's scent and women's mix in my blest air.

11

There are no sorrows wine cannot allay.
There are no sins wine cannot wash away.
No riddles too obscure for wine to read.
No debts too onerous for wine to pay.

12

Would you forget a woman? Drink bright wine.
Would you remember her? Drink this bright wine.
Is your heart breaking for a glimpse of her?
Gaze deep into this mirror of bright wine.

13

Were I a woman, I might all day through
Gaze at my glass, uncertain what to do;
And, catching some particular deep look,
Think to myself, 'Can I be really you?'

14

The wine-cup is a wistful magic glass
In which all day lost looks return and pass.
Dead lips kiss ours upon the scented brim,
And whisper messages, and smile, and pass.

15

Shall I, with such a paltry hoard to spend,
Waste it to an unprofitable end?
Do as you please who think another way.
For me, the wine-cup and the more-than-friend.

55

16

Don't think that I have never tried your way
To heaven, you who pray and fast and pray.
Once I denied myself both love and wine –
For one incomparably dreadful day.

17

The right book, the right woman, and good wine –
And Heaven is here. Perhaps your highest shrine
Is some bare place of singing sour and cold –
But when did I last claim your Heaven was mine?

18

You to the mosque, with howling hymn and prayer,
I to the temple of the vine repair,
The one true God in divers ways to seek.
I find him here – friend, do you find him there?

19

How many of the pious who cry shame,
With holy horror, on our tattered fame,
Watch only for the opportunity
Of turned backs and the dark – to do the same?

20

And what care I for what the Sufis say?
The Sufis are but drunk another way.
So you be drunk, it matters not the means.
Try not to laugh at *others* as they sway.

21

But what is there to win that is not mine?
This bottle, friend, is still half-full of wine.
Despite my sins, soft forms approach me yet.
What better winnings, pious friend, are thine?

22

To all of us the thought of heaven is dear –
So, let's be sure of it, and make it here.
Perhaps there is a heaven yonder too;
But why take needless risks, with you so near?

23

Eternal torment some grim skulls foretell
For those who worship wine and love too well.
Yet, God would quit the dull companionship
Of Heaven, if all the drinkers were in Hell.

24

If it's a sin to drink the golden wine,
The sin is surely His, not yours or mine.
Fated to drink, how dare I disobey?
How *can* I counterwork the law divine?

25

God gave me eyesight – shall I rob my eyes?
He gave me sense, instead of merchandise.
Why should such subtle shapes exist as do,
And not be there for me to recognise?

26

Allah, that numbers all my whitening hairs,
Knows, without telling, all my tiny cares.
Allah is grateful. He will not forget
I have not wearied him with endless prayers.

27

I am not fit for hell – I am too small.
Eternity can have no cause to call
On such an insignificance as me.
I am too poor a prey for it to maul.

57

28

Great prophets and great princes, it may be,
Dare hope to sin to such a great degree
That God is forced to punish them for ever.
Distinction far too great for such as we.

29

The Hell-believer who yet knows Thy grace
Shall surely find in Hell his resting-place.
Fit but for mosques these fables of Thy wrath –
No man believes them who has seen Thy face.

30

Yet, stay. What man has seen thy face indeed?
Why should a world where thousands flail and bleed
Not prove a telling sample of thy kindness?
To hope for more is surely hellish greed?

31

For he was hardly forced to make us. So
The world's rich natural expanse of woe
Is quite superfluous. All made by him
For motives which we don't presume to know.

32

So, since for all my passion and my skill,
The world's profound intent eludes me still,
Must I not piously believe that I
Am kept in darkness by the heavenly will?

33

Into this life of cruel wonder sent,
Without a word to tell us what it meant;
Sent back again without a reason heard –
Birth, life and death – and all half-bafflement.

34

And do you think that unto such as you,
A maggot-minded, starved, fanatic crew,
God gave the Secret, and denied it me?
Dear, blessed fools! Go on. Believe that too.

35

All wrong; all wrong. All in the end are wrong.
No-one hears all the music of the song.
A few notes here are caught; a few notes there.
But even these few notes none can hold for long.

36

The Koran! Well, come put me to the test –
Mighty old book in thrilling errors dressed –
Believe me, I have read the Koran too.
The unbelievers know the Koran best.

37

If I were God, I would not wait for years
To solve the mystery of human tears.
I would reveal my will, Godlike, to all –
Not hint it darkly to some dreaming seers.

38

Allah, perhaps, the secret word might spell.
If He exists, he keeps his secret well.
And who shall hope to find what He has hidden?
Shall God his answers to a maggot tell?

39

What the great secret is never appears.
Explicitness is rarely found in seers.
Too drunk with joy to tell us what they tasted –
The cloud that masks their sun never quite clears.

40

You want to know the secret – so did I;
Low in the dust I sought it, and on high
Chased it in awful flight from star to star.
Yet: what was I supposed to know it by?

41

Up, up, where Parwin's hoofs stamp heaven's floor,
My soul went knocking at each starlit door;
Till on the silent top of heaven's stair,
Clear-eyed, I looked – and laughed – and climbed no more.

42

No! think no more, but grip the slender waist
Of her whose kisses leave no bitter taste.
Enjoy the help that lingers in such warmth.
Such blissful trust can never be misplaced.

43

Ask me no more about three, four, and five.
Is it not strange enough to be alive?
Ah! How profoundly we may chase that thought –
Deeper than any trap you might contrive.

44

Look not above: there is no answer there.
No-one is interested in your prayer.
Near is no nearer God than any far.
And Here is just the same deceit as There.

45

In all those star-cold heavens shall we find
Another home, so safe, so green and kind?
No, we shall not. Come, fill another glass.
No second home, and no inquiring mind.

46

But here is wine; here kind and lovely girls.
Be wise, and drown your sorrows in their curls.
Dive all you will in life's disrupting seas,
You shall not find more covetable pearls.

47

O speak no evil of these dancing flowers;
These girls that arrogantly we call ours –
The tinkling of the bangles on their wrists
Should sound like wisdom to the Higher Powers.

48

I would not change the song the flute-girl sings
For all the diadems of weary kings.
This delicate young hand against my chest;
My own enchanted by so many things.

49

Let those of us who think this life is best
Not, craven, lie about it like the rest.
But lift our glasses frankly to the sun;
And clasp our loves as frankly to our breast.

50

Not all the fancies of the devotee
Shall make fair pleasure less than fair for me.
These things are good: this her, this wine, this music.
Should I exchange them for hypocrisy?

51

Here is the creed of Omar: I believe
In old wine and good new wine; I believe
In well-formed women, whether old or new;
And in the world that made them I believe.

52

If only this green world might last for ever!
And girls be girls, and wine be wine for ever!
I ask for nothing more than what I have.
Only – that I might keep it here for ever!

53

Oh, love, love, love – come, let us drink for joy!
I am no corpse, and you no pointless boy!
Precariousness so near on every side.
Your tongue moves, and the world becomes a toy.

54

Core of my heart, in such an hour as this
The cup of life brims near too full of bliss;
My joy exceeds the boundaries of my heart.
The earth must all transform when next we kiss.

55

My dazzled eyes scarce dare believe you here.
I'm half afraid to blink them, I so fear,
When they re-open, I shall be alone.
Nearer, my love, oh nearer, now, more near.

56

Oh love, how right the world, how bright the sky!
And we are living – *living* – you and I!
For this is life – this *is* life, is it not?
How good to live before we're fit to die!

57

Shall death, that shuts the ear and locks the brain,
Teach us what eager life has sought in vain?
The rotting fingers of the skeleton
Grasp what the living hand could not contain?

58

When this mysterious self shall leave behind
The subtle clay supposed to keep it blind,
There soon will be real silence in the room,
And no-one notice a departing mind.

59

Such lovely women now lie underground.
Such mighty heroes now lie underground.
And nothing moves there; nothing makes a sound –
Except for countless beasts now underground.

60

One bubble's but a bubble – and a pair
Is but a pair of transients in the air.
A bubble's life – what can it mean to him?
A million bubbles burst. What does he care?

61

Some say we came God's purpose to fulfil –
A paltry purpose, then; a feeble will.
Sport for the heavenly huntsmen, others claim –
So lame a sport requires but little skill.

62

How strange the pattern of this life of ours!
Who knows the meaning of the heavenly powers?
Great Caesar's wounds bleed yearly in the roses,
And flower-like ladies fade and turn to flowers.

63

Each day falls gold or withered from the tree
Whose leaves make up the life of you and me;
To join the others heaped upon the earth,
Stretching beyond what any eyes can see.

64

And all who in their graves unheeded lie
Were just as hungry once as you and I.
They clucked their vanished, endless syllables,
Nodded their heads, and scarcely thought to die.

65

What long-dead face makes this grass here so green?
On whose earth-buried bosom do we lean?
Ah, love! when we in turn are flowers and grass,
By what unseeing eyes shall we be seen?

66

A beauty lies beneath yon surging grass
Whom once I thought the world could not surpass.
Beside her lies a later and a lovelier.
Over all this, one breath whispers, 'Alas'.

67

At times, this world seems as a dream that cries
In fancy's ears and lives in fancy's eyes.
The dreamed solutions to dreamed questionings.
We dream we find, and dream that we are wise.

68

For even the dust that blows along the street
Once whispered to its love that life was sweet,
And slipped through quiet gates to secret meetings,
Though now you bless it with your hurrying feet.

69

Passionate particles of dust and sun,
Run your brief race, nor ask why it is run –
We are all shadow-pictures, voices, dreams.
Perhaps for purposes; perhaps for fun.

64

70

Lost to a world in which I crave no part,
I sit alone and listen to my heart;
Pleased with my little corner of the earth –
Glad to be here, glad that I shall depart.

71

And to my solitude I sometimes bring
An aiding shape to sit with me and sing –
A music in her presence as her voice –
And all need drowned for any other thing.

72

Why should it be that those who merit least
Must be the normal masters of the feast?
Yet, I, whom one companion sates, will leave them
To sad bouts, which must ever be increased.

73

Strange, that a world so wonderfully planned
Should often let a halfwit rule our land.
Ah well, the cup must solve that riddle too.
It's more than I shall ever understand.

74

Have I not wine, this friend to drink with me,
This garden, and this gracious company
Of thought and beauty, and that rising planet?
I envy those who do not envy me.

75

Set not your heart on final good or gain;
Life means but pleasure, or it means but pain.
When Time unlocks a little perfect hour,
Enter it – for it will not come again.

76

The bird of life is singing on the bough
His two eternal notes of 'I' and 'Thou' –
Oh listen! for the song so soon sings through.
If we would hear it, we must hear it now.

77

Good friends, take care! the only life we know
Flies from us like an arrow from the bow,
While life, a moving target, hurries by.
Shoot now! For things will not be always so.

78

The bird of life is singing in the sun;
Short is his song, and now it has begun –
A trill, a call, a rapture, then – so soon! –
It breaks off, scarce observed by anyone.

79

Can we accept the fleeting time that's ours?
Today, this view. Tomorrow, shuttered bowers.
Here in the meadow for an arc of summer,
Only a brief while longer than the flowers.

80

Would you be happy? When? Oh, hear my way:
Forget tomorrow, heed not yesterday.
The only words of life are, *here* and *now*.
All others are diversion and delay.

81

Only a little safer than the blooms,
We sit in gardens or stride through our rooms,
For decade after decade after decade,
Before – alas! how soon! – we fill our tombs.

66

82

And even then – who knows? – we'll meet again,
Nor the celestial wine-cup cease to drain,
And in some unreal, laughing heaven elsewhere
Small loving women to our bodies strain.

83

I sometimes doubt that the Beloved Friend
Who made the world so fair, would gladly rend
This lovely curtain of the night and day
To tatters, which he *never* means to mend.

84

Life is too short, my dear one, for despair.
The outburst of a moment beats the air.
Better a cry of happiness than rage.
But silence follows both, and does not care.

85

And if the soul should with the body die –
The flame still flickers as the oil runs dry.
Yet, where's the flame beyond the final drop?
And what remains of this you once called 'I'?

86

But don't expect poor Khayyam to make plain
Great riddles to your nobly prying brain;
Who stops to marvel at a subtle whorl,
And stares in wonder at the absent rain.

87

When to the loot of life I sidle near,
Hoping to lift a little worldly gear,
I find that dolts have carted off the best,
Leaving me only – year succeeding year.

67

88

Like a timid bird, my life has flown away.
I heard him sing all morning long in May,
And was convinced his song could never end.
I was convinced, and yet: he did not stay.

89

So, now what profit to my bruised estate
If the abodes of bliss be seven or eight?
Reach me but wine to soothe me where I lie,
Heart-broken, stretched upon the wheel of Fate.

90

To me there is much comfort in the thought
That all our agonies can alter nought.
Our lives are written to their final word.
We but repeat a lesson HE has taught.

91

Yet, I concede my masochistic taint.
For, though I think, as well befits a saint,
That all of us are tortured in Heaven's dungeon,
I grant that some might find such comfort *faint*.

92

Khayyam, who long at learning's tents has sewn,
Bids you to leave the HOW and WHY alone.
Iram's soft instrument of dampened joy
Will tell you most that ever can be known.

93

How strange man is, that can forget so soon
The daily wonder of the sun and moon;
And his deep heart on pointless riddles breaks,
Instead of sporting morn and afternoon.

68

94
Who finds a meaning in a grain of sand
Knows the whole meaning of the sea and land;
A simple one by thousands multiplied
Is no more possible to understand.

95
We ask and ask; and where real questions lie
We may succeed, or fail, before we die;
But All-That-Is is not a question – more
A statement. How then are we to reply?

96
Passionate particles of dust and sun,
Run your brief race, for races should be run.
If we are only shadows, voices, dreams –
Whose are the purposes? Whose is the fun?

97
Timid at crossroads, with what fear we try
To find the better road ahead – but why?
All earthly roads lead nowhere at the last.
What matters then the road we travel by?

98
Would we were sure of some oasis blest,
Where, the long journey over, we might rest.
Then, just to sleep for an eternity
Were Paradise, within the earth's dark breast!

99
Of all my seeking this is all my gain:
No agony of any mortal brain
Shall wrest a secret of the life of Man.
The search has taught me that the search is vain.

100

For we should see the journey as the end.
There is no destination. Thus, O friend,
Seek out the best, most honourable route,
And those you meet may on your worth depend.

101

For, though the flowers frame your flowering head,
And sinuously your sinuous limbs you spread,
Not even you are gold. We can't expect
That men will dig us up when we are dead.

102

Write it in wine upon a rose-leaved scroll:
All wisdom I found hidden in the bowl.
All answers to my questions, saving one –
How is the body different from the soul?

103

How desperately some expect the dead
To answer their wild questions in their stead;
The empty space within the rotting skull
Prove more capacious than the living head!

104

Mysterious mother substance, who are they
That scorn the earth which made them? Who are they
That waste their wonder on imagined souls?
I marvel at this arrogance of clay.

105

This clay, so strong of heart, of sense so fine –
Surely such clay is near enough divine!
Only a fool speaks evil of the clay.
The very stars are made of clay like mine!

106

This clay, this dream-sown turf, this chymic earth;
This wizard dust, wherein all kinds of birth –
Small buds, huge beasts, and undecided princes –
Mute seeds of wonder, fill a needle's girth.

107

This clay, this haunted house of sight and sound –
Strange sunny rooms that airily resound
With phantom music played for phantom feet –
While rats gnaw, large and silent, underground.

108

For mark yon potter! See the rascal twirl
On one base wheel the dust of prince and churl;
Kneading the brains of forty dead desires
To make an ointment-jar for someone's girl.

109

The laughter from an empire now decayed;
The secret strains where so much music played;
More beauty than a lifetime can contain –
And, look! this fellow turns it to a trade!

110

And as I spoke I heard a whisper steal,
Like sad low laughter, from the potter's wheel –
Behold! it was my father's sacred dust,
Amused that I esteemed myself more real.

111

Great Potter, on whose tool, a wheeling blue,
The world is fashioned and is broken too –
Why to the race of men is heaven so dire?
In what, Great Tool, have we offended you?

112

Beautiful wheel of blue above my head,
Will you be turning still when I am dead?
Were you yet turning long before I came?
Khayyam, the bowl is empty – go to bed.

113

I am not really sorry I was born.
Though my estate be poor, my garments torn,
And all who pass regard me as a fool.
No. No: not *really* sorry I was born.

114

At the pale gate of birth an angel stands
Singing a lying song of lovely lands;
We listen for too long to what he says,
And life, real life, slips each day through our hands.

115

Would that some voice which knew the whole deceit
Far off in space the unborn soul might greet,
Hot-foot for earth, with lying fancies fired,
And blurt out all the terror and the cheat.

116

But what real thing could such a spirit be?
How far in space? What would be there to see?
We live in life; and not before or after;
And what scares some need not dispirit me.

117

Nor are those sightless stars a whit more wise –
Impotent silver dots upon the dies
The lords of heaven each night and morning throw,
In some peculiar hazard of the skies.

72

118

Let us make haste, perchance for us to warn
The eager soul that clamours to be born;
To rescue them from their tremendous doom,
Those fated generations still unborn.

119

Perchance to warn? And yet – for whom the warning?
What odd realm are these unborn souls adorning?
Fate's but a name for anything that happens.
Nothing can waken in an unborn morning.

120

Men talk of heaven – there is no heaven but here.
Men talk of hell – there is no hell but here.
Men talk of pasts. Men talk of what's to come.
Yet, all this talk is but two words: *Now. Here.*

121

And when at last the shrouded saki, Death,
Brings me a cup so sweet it halts my breath,
Shall I not bid him welcome like his brother?
I have not feared Life; shall I then fear Death?

122

Nor yet shall fail the efficacious Vine:
Wash me as pure as silver in old wine,
And for my coffin fragrant timbers take
Of tendrilled wood – then plant a rose; then dine!

123

O friends, forget not, as you laugh and play,
Some that were laughing with you yesterday.
Sprinkle some wine upon the parching clay,
And *then* forget them – they're too far away.

73

124
There is no greater piety than this:
To set aside a little of your bliss
Between potations, to recall the dead;
And look condignly solemn as you piss.

125
Such are the thoughts the dead would think upon.
Warm in the sun the kind old world spins on,
Trellised with vines and females as of old,
And no-one asks, 'Where is old Khayyam gone?'

126
A wild life, but a sweet one, saintly brother;
Nor in this harsh world know I such another.
Illicit? Ah, how often we prefer
The silly daughter to the clever mother.

127
Only a breath divides belief from doubt;
The muttered breath that makes a man devout.
Only a breath divides a life from death.
A mere breath, yet so many scream and shout.

128
At Ramadan, the pleasant days are done.
Then pious breath obscures the very sun.
Wine mopes neglected in its jars, and women
Vanish as if a charm had been unspun.

129
But let me fall upon the instant dead
When some exquisite creature turns her head
Towards me, in an elegant, warm glance,
And I should fail to hear what's being said.

74

130

Then were it time indeed to say goodbye
To the green earth and the old happy sky:
Bury me quick, a love-devoid old corpse;
There's now no more of Khayyam left to die.

131

No-one can claim that I have turned away,
Ungrateful, when some woman asked me stay.
I tried to do what was required; and that
Is more than most of our Sultans can say.

132

Oh, must the blithely wise be sent to school
For ever to the narrow-minded fool?
The evil-smelling saint outlaw the flowers?
The joyful pale beneath a joyless rule?

133

Yet, sometimes, of a sudden all seems clear –
Now! Hush, my soul! The Secret draws so near.
Make silence ready for the speech divine.
If Heaven should speak, and no-one want to hear!

134

Yes! Sometimes on the instant all seems plain.
The simple sun could tell us, or the rain.
The world, caught dreaming with a look of heaven,
At last seems almost ready) to explain.
Seems on a sudden tip-toe)

135

As a young beauty, tantalising, turns
A face that promises to him who burns
To hear her answer – so the world tricks all,
And hints at truths which no man ever learns.

136
As Spring now cuckoo-sobs deep in its throat;
Over the land his thrilling whispers float.
Old earth believes its thrilling lies once more,
And runs to meet him in a golden coat.

137
And many a lovely girl that long has lain
Beneath the grass, moved by the sun and rain,
Lifts up a blossomed head to hear him sing,
Listens (what nonsense!), smiles, and sleeps again.

138
How often have these petals gone the way
Of might and beauty; yet, those went to stay,
Whereas the roses have returned to us;
Back in our world, with what strange scents to say.

139
With twilight dew each flower's face is wet;
Morning was bright upon them when we met –
Was that indeed one whole day passed? No matter.
There's many a useful hour till bed-time yet.

140
Night with a sudden splendour opens wide
Her purple robe, and bares her dazzling side;
The moon, her bosom, fills the world with light –
Only by your half-hidden breasts outvied.

141
How delicate the moon appears; how high.
We crane our heads together, you and I.
Some kindly structure of the universe
Has echoed you so gently in the sky.

142

The moon so lovely – does it make me dote?
I turn my head, and watch a woman's throat,
Talking beside me in the early night;
Amazed one is so near; one so remote.

143

Dear friend, when I at last have run my race,
Will you remember my accustomed place
When through the garden the long summer night
The moon goes seeking my forgotten face?

144

Ah yes! If somewhere at the journey's end
Friend might again behold the face of friend!
But how forgetful of us grow the dead,
That never word or whisper to us send.

145

Where are the fair old faces: gone, or hiding?
Where is the far-off place of their abiding?
I asked the wise, and thus the wise replied:
'Drink, my friend, drink. They're gone beyond all tiding.'

146

When, with wild joys and sorrows broken quite,
I face the glad dawn of my endless night,
Still shall I call for wine, and still for you,
Till pleasure close the eyes she once kept bright.

147

Impassioned particles of dirt and sun,
Run your brief race, if one is being run.
Are we but shadows? Yet: I heard your laughter.
Don't say we had no purpose. I had one.

148

There are few sorrows love cannot allay.
There are few sins love cannot wash away.
Few riddles too obscure for love to read.
No debts too onerous for love to pay.

149

Love, the fair day is drawing to a close.
The stars are rising, while a soft wind blows.
The doors of heaven are opening in a dream –
Let us watch silent till again they close.

150

How wonderfully has our day gone by!
If only as the stars come we could die,
And morning find us gathered to our dreams –
(Two happy solemn faces and the sky.
(Two faces fading gladly into the (gold sky.
                                        (fresh